SIMPLY PUT!

A Message To Young Black Brothers In The "Free World" And To Those Who Are Incarcerated

By
Kareem Tomblin

PriorityBooks PUBLICATIONS

P.O. Box 2535

Florissant, Mo 63033

Edited by: Brenda Matthews and Kendra Koger

Cover Designed by Sheldon Mitchell of Majaluk

All scriptures are taken from thc King James Version of the Bible.

Manufactured in the United States of America

Library of Congress Control Number: 2009911086

ISBN: 9780981991337

For information regarding discounts for bulk purchases, please contact Prioritybooks Publications at www.prioritybooks.com or rosbeav03@yahoo.com.

SIMPLY PUT!

A Message To Young Black Brothers In The "Free World"
And To Those Who Are Incarcerated

by Kareem Tomblin

Published by
Prioritybooks Publications Missouri

Contents

Dedication:

I dedicate *Simply Put* to all of my young black brothers incarcerated who are striving hard to change for the better.

Acknowledgements:

First and foremost, I must thank the good Lord above for showering me continuously with His grace and love. Lord God, you have been with me since birth. You were even there when I was hustling drugs. It was You who kept me protected, not the guns I carried, or the rugged tough attitude I possessed as a thug; I could never-ever repay you for all that you have done. But I will always bless Your name from the rising and going down of the sun. You alone are wonderful. Thank You for Your blessings.

To: My dear mother "Geneva", who is beyond doubt the greatest woman I know, I love you. Above all though, thank you for your many, many prayers.

To: Rose J. Beavers, I thank you sistah for believing in a brutha. You are a very gracious woman and I appreciate you.

To: Adrian Davis, Donald Thomas, Reddy Mike, Timothy Fewell, J. Beckham, L. Lucas, Tommy, Anthony Cannon, D. Lucas, Mr. David Stephen Rollison, young "Gist", Lil Kareem, Big Bro. Grove and Lil Bro. Grove, Anthony Williamson, "Cuzo", Big R. Potts, Jerome, Eimmis, Dobbie, Yo-Yo, All of my nieces – nephews – aunts – cousins, J. Daniels, Kevin Bullock, Lil "T. Scott", D. White (Lyfe), Jackie, Katherine Johnson, Marshay, Tiffany Mungo (What up Queen? Or shall I say, Rider?) , Ms. Wanda (sorry for getting caught in your house when I was young. I, along with your daughter thought we were grown. I apologize.), A. Stowe (Tee), Schoolboy, James D. Sarratt, Jacques Floyd, Antonio J. (Co-writer of "A Knock At Midnight". Dawg you like that!), my lil bro. "Q", "Man-Man" (Va.) (You owe me), Toine (Va.), Chris, Big Lou (DC), Jeffery Arnold, Duke and lil Git, All my Queen City homies. (Yo', y'all too damn numerous to name. But I love ya'), Monique Hall (You made it through prison, now you gotta show the world that the time you spent wasn't in vain, sistah. Holla at me.), Cousin Steve (Thank you for praying for me.), Annette

(Thank you for sticking by me. You are a true family member.) And, to everyone else who keeps it real at all times with me, I appreciate you. Oh yeah, C. Meadows, Ru-Ru, Big Leroy, Jay-Row, SB (Girly you shoulda been a model. You are so beautiful and cute). Booker Gattis (Stay focused bro., and write. You're too talented to play around with your skills). Thurston and Big King (Thank y'all brothers for helping brothers in prison with law work.), K. Wingate (Every time I see you, you're teaching and helping brothers get their G.E.D., whatever you do, don't stop. You're very important). Also, a special shout out to "Rock" and "Dre" from the barbershop here in Bennettsville.

Lastly, but certainly not least: I want to give a very, very special shout out to "Christan". Little brother, your mother talks about you all the time. She says that you're going to be a "doctor". I want you to know that I salute you. Even though you don't have your father in your life, you are not using that as an excuse to fail in life. You are a young man of "vision", and that's important to have, because as the Bible says, WITHOUT A VISION THE PEOPLE WILL PERISH!" Continue to stay focused young brother.

To: Darius Phillips, Uncle Snoop loves you, never doubt that! Jasper Allen (What up, boy?)

I would like to also say thank you to Soledad O'Brien of CNN for the inspiration she has given me through her special documentary, Black In America 1 & 2.

Finally, I want to thank Brenda Hampton, Keisha Ervin, Tigner (Savannah, Georgia), Bobby Digital (What up fam?), U-god (Quit playin' boy!), OOSAONLINEBOOKCLUB for their support. Thank you Hamm (What up Elder?), Brother Lester (Keep being about God's business!), Brother Monroe, Brother Billy, and all my brothers in Christ, (Continue to let Christ use you!) and Brother Taureece (Keep your head up, Warrior!)

Foreward

Knowledge Breeds Power For Real

In almost every circle of professionals, educators, and pastors, this question is sure to come up as to 'why African American males are not making it in society." Another question pondered is why are our young men dropping out of school? Especially since it is proven that without an education in this time and age, life can seem pretty bleak. Yet, still they drop out of school around the 9th grade. You figure, if a person can't get a job with a high school diploma, what in the world can they do with a 9th grade education. Yet by the hundreds they still dropout. Education is very important. When people lack education you can almost predict where their lives will end up without intervention.

African American males are in a crisis. They are dropping out of school and ending up in jail, while others are finding themselves on the short end of the stick of not having employment opportunities. I believe that if someone wants to beat the negative disadvantages they have to put in the work by going to school and college. I also believe that self esteem issues need to be addressed with our young men which if increased can change their lives. Black males can beat the statistics but it will take perseverance and a change of attitude.

So what if our young men happened to find themselves in jail because they didn't listen? Hopefully now they will utilize this time to do something useful like get a diploma or go to school to get a degree. Why waste time in jail not educating yourself? Isn't the lack of knowledge what put you in this place?" Without an education you can't win. If you follow the wrong crowd, you may end up in jail or prison and bad choices leads to no where? All these things happen because of a lack of knowledge. The

Bible says that without knowledge our people will perish. So why continue downhill?

According to a report by the Pew Center on the States' Public Safety Performance Project, at the start of 2008, 2,319,258 adults were held in American prisons or jails or one in every 99.1 men and women, according to the study. As prison populations expand, costs to states are on the rise. With all the money being spent, the national recidivism rate remains virtually unchanged, with about half of released inmates returning to jail or prison within three years.

Why do you think more than half of the inmates return to prison? Could it be that prisoners are not investing in themselves while being locked up? What do you think would happen if prisoners went to school and received their General Education Diploma or achieve a higher degree? Do you think that with education people prosper? I do! I am a firm believer that education really does breed knowledge and help people to make better choices about where their lives are headed.

This is why I am happy to write this forward for Kareem Tomblin. He has spent so many years in prison but he has put in a lot of work to educate and enlighten himself. His desire is that youths will make better choices so that they will not end up in prison as he did. Still, if our young men failed to heed to warnings by those who love them the most while on the outside, maybe they'll listen to someone who is on the inside. Kareem is asking that prisoners put in the time to educate themselves so that when the time comes for them to re-enter society, they will have educated themselves to do better, thus helping to drop the recidivism rate. After all, an educated mind can change things.

It is hard today trying to inspire people to use every advantage that they have now to become successful. Too many people from teachers, pastors and ministers, parents, friends, volunteers, and others work many hours trying to instill hope and inspiration when many of our teens possess so much hopelessness. But educating yourself can inspire hope, help you to gain a job, increase your self esteem and change the way others see you. The book *Simply Put* is a simple request by the author to change your life by educating yourself and making change for the betterment of our communities, families, and for self. It is Kareem's hope that people will not end up as he did because he was an uneducated young man. It ıs his testimony that education breeds knowledge and that knowledge breeds positive self esteem and with each of these you can change your circumstances.

I fully recommend that all teens read this book because they can change their lives by staying in school and not end up in the prison system but in the college system. Further, I thank Kareem for inspiring our brothers and sisters who are in prison so that they will know that all is not lost if they invest in themselves by taking full advantage of the education opportunities while they are incarcerated.

Rose Jackson-Beavers
Author and Publisher

A Special Call to Action

Black Men Where Are You?!

By now, I'm sure that many of you have heard about the recent beating of the teenager in Chicago, many have seen the school bus incident where two Black teenage students attacked a white student, and just last night in my hometown, another 16 year old was gunned down by his peers. This is happening everywhere, and unless we begin to address the real reasons as to why this is happening, more of our children will be killed. Just think, what if something like what happened to Derrion Albert happened to your sons or daughters? I've thought about it, and the thought pains me. I can't even imagine what the mothers and fathers go through after losing their children, but after watching the video of Derrion Albert being beat, I can't rest peacefully and I'm literally sick to my stomach. I can't stop thinking about how anyone can cause such harm to another person. What's going on with *you*, where *you* feel proud about stomping someone to death or bashing their head in? Right now, I won't even comment on what I feel for those who were arrested, but I will tell you that I have very little remorse for them. Maybe I should feel sorry for them too, after all, they were taught how to approach life by their mothers or maybe...fathers?

By the way, Dad, where are you? Your sons NEED you! Don't you get it? They...we are all crying out for your help! Mom just can't do it alone anymore, and even though many women do a great job raising their children as single parents, obviously, some women don't! Either way, Dad, when are you going to take responsibility for bringing a human being into this world? You just can't walk away and think that your kids do not need you. Your daughters NEED you too, and every time she searches for love in the wrong place, she's really looking for you. Your sons...oh, my

God, please help your sons! Go get them from our streets, and stop them from killing each other. Stop them from overcrowding our prisons and being made examples of. Let them know there's a sensible way to approach life. Put your arms around them and tell them that you're sorry for abandoning them. Tell them that you love them, that you're proud of them and that you're willing to do whatever it takes to make their lives better. Don't wait for another man, a mentor, the president, or any other male figure to do it. Think about it...he's got your blood running through his body and he will carry on the legacy that you taught him. Have you asked yourself what you want your legacy to be? Please, give him a chance that you are failing to give him. Wherever your children may be, find them; connect with them, talk to them, be there for them, please! There is no other way for anyone to correct what is going on, if you do not make an effort to do your part.

What we're watching play out in the streets of our cities are the results of continuous neglect from parents, particularly fathers. Now is the time, and we can't afford to wait another hour, day or years for certain individuals to step up. The mission starts with you and you know who you are. Close the doors to your weak ways of thinking and realize how much difference it would make if you gave your children the time they truly deserve. I know change isn't easy and it brings about many challenges. Set aside your fears. To prevent us from losing more of our precious children, please, black men especially, do the right thing. At the end of the day, Derrion Albert and all of the other innocent children who have lost their lives, didn't deserve to be taken away from us by the young men some of us are creating. If any of these children belong to you, think about their future, your future, and the future you could have allowed Derrion Albert to have, had you been there for your child. Remember, it's not too late to make sure this doesn't happen to another innocent victim.

Brenda Hampton
Essence Magazine Bestselling Author
www.brendamhampton. com

Novels:
Two Wrongs Don't Make a Right
The Dirty Truth
SLICK
How Can I Be Down?
No Justice No Peace
The Naughty Series
Girls From Da Hood 5-Trick Don't Treat

IGNORANCE is a cure for nothing!

W.E.B. Dubois

FIRST & FOREMOST!

Dear Young Brother

Dear "You," my young brother:

I know that you do not know me personally, nor I, you. If you are out there in your neighborhood "thuggin" and just straight up and out being a menace, then you are my concern, and I would like to speak to you from my heart because we are family. Yes, you are my little brother and as one of your "big brothers," it is my duty and assignment by birthright to help you see your way through the fog of the underworld life. The ways of thuggism only leads to prison or buried six feet deep underground in someone's cemetery – usually and sadly, at a young age!

As one of your big brothers, who is a little wiser, nothing means more to me than reaching you before you self-destruct! It has come to my attention that many of you want to be like the rappers you see on BET (Buster Entertainment Television!). Buster Entertainment Television is what I rightly call BET because no real concern about what you view on a television "station" would allow FAKE Jeezy, FAKE Lil Wayne, FAKE Rick Ross, and them cats, to continue poisoning its young listeners with the garbage that these FAKE-PHONY-WANNABE "gangstahs" and "thug" rappers keep spitting in the ears of young brothers who have the potential to be the next Barack Obama. At the same time, easily led astray by these "busters" who are already rich, but still refuse to abandon rapping about a "game" that's long been over! (The drug game!)

Little brother, listen to me because I know what it's like to be a thug – first class! I also know what it's like to nearly lose your life in the process or in the alternative, receive more time to serve in a federal prison than you can bare, literally!

The government arrested me and fourteen other young thugs in the year of 1992 for kidnapping drug dealers, robbing and killing them, seriously maiming others and selling narcotics such as cocaine and heroin. The government alleged that my co-conspirators and I did all those things in order to support and maintain our organization called "NBC" (NIGGAS Being Crucial!) The term NIGGAS meant, Never Ignorant Getting Goals Accomplished! The government also referred to my co-conspirators and me collectively as The West Charlotte Posse because that was the area we took over. When the government arrested us, I was the youngest of the bunch. I was 17 years olds... At 18 years old, I was on my way to prison. Not to one of those "kitty camps" where everything is "all gravy" and "sweet." No... I was sent to a Maximum Security Prison called "the penitentiary," where the government sends people like mob bosses, major drug kingpins, hit men, gang chiefs, and the hardest of criminals! I was sent to a place like that with 540 months to serve. If you haven't ignorantly dropped out of school, like most thugs do, and can count, then you know that 540 months equal up to "45" years. And, in the federal system you have to do at least 85 percent of your prison time before you can be eligible for release. So, hey, you do the math!

Upon arrival, I had to start carrying a "shank" (prison made knife) for protection because when you are young and fresh in the penal system, some sick minded person who may have been locked up damn near all of his life and looking for some "fresh meat" may step to you to see what you're made of. If you are soft, you may end up with a thick penis up your virgin anus! So, in a place like this, where either you fight, take flight, or get f*#@ed, that's the way it is, and what you will have to deal with!

I have broken my hand in bloody fist fights here, and I have busted heads with broom sticks! I came in the system a man, and that's how I will leave... So, young brother, I know all about being hard and being a thug! And you know what? If I had to do it all over again, I would have stayed my backside in school and far away from the underworld of the streets. However, as I was saying earlier brother, the Lil Waynes; the Jeezys; the Rick Rosses and them cats are phony gangstahs and thugs. When you hear them rappin' about selling drugs and poppin' guns and whatnot, ask yourself, young brother, this simple question: WHY AREN'T THESE RAPPERS SOMEWHERE UNDER INDICTMENT BY THE "FEDS" OR SOMEWHERE LOCKED UP!?

Use your head and ask yourself this because these days the Federal Government is the biggest and meanest gang in town. They know who's doing what especially if it's illegal and on the major scale that these rappers swear that they are on. First and foremost, no real true gangstah or harden thug will ever broadcast underworld business. Putting your dirty laundry out to air for everyone's nostrils to smell is not the gangstah or thug way. One of the first things one learns in the streets is to keep his/her mouth shut because "loose lips sink ships!" The Feds will lock you up and throw away the key if they get the slightest hint that a person is selling the quantity of coke and heroin some of these so called thug, gangstah, organized crime lords that rappers want you to believe they are hustling in their hood and across their city.

One rapper I was listening to claim he got them "thangz" (kilos) going for $17,5000. Another, as phony as him, claim to get them thangz at "ten-a-key" (ten thousand dollars per kilo).

Brothers, if these cats are in the "game" like that in which I know they are not because I know a counterfeit when I see and hear one, they would be right here where I am. If these clown rappers are real, what would make them different from the guys who are in here serving major time for being deep in the game? How are they different from those who got snitched on and aggressively prosecuted by the Feds? Are these phony rappers telling us that they are untouchable? Because if that's what they are telling us, then what makes them different from Leroy Nicky Barnes? He was the figure head for an alleged underworld crime family called the Council, a group of organized black men responsible for flooding the streets of Harlem with heroin.

Brothers, Leroy Nicky Barnes made millions with his friends and associates and he was said to have been called "Mr. Untouchable." That is, until the Feds came down hard on him and burst his bubble! When the Feds came down hard on Leroy Nicky Barnes, brothers, guess what he did? He "ratted" on all of the guys he made major money with. Some of these guys were his closest friends.

All big drug boys like Jeezy and Rick Ross who claims that they are, have crews of dudes working for them because no one man can move major quantities of drugs alone.

In every crew, trust me, somebody is a "weak-link" and a weak link is someone who can't or refuse to keep his/her mouth shut about underworld affairs. When underworld figures start running their mouths to the police about what they were accomplishing while in the game and who they were accomplishing these things with, that's when kingdoms fall and the FEDS start passing out life sentences to all corporates involved as a result! Next to death, prison is a drug dealer's fate, no exception!

The point that I'm making is: these rappers who you may idolize and want to be just like are no more than "studio gangstahs," and "studio thugs." At the end of the day, after they leave the studio, go back to the comforts of their big houses on a hill, far away from the hood, and far away from a corner selling cocaine. They are playing with their children, enjoying their normal lives. Many of you, my young brothers, can't distinguish between fact and fiction. It takes someone who loves you a lot and don't want to see you dead or in prison, with a lot of time to do, to help open your eyes to what's real and what's phony. BET (Buster Entertainment Television), doesn't care about you so they are not gonna stop to explain the truth to you. All they want is for you to keep viewing their programs. They know you like that hard street stuff so they give it to you on a platter...fake or not!

Then, you go out into your community, cop you a gun and some dope, forget all about school, and start thuggin uncompromisingly in your hood. You start thuggin so hard that no one can seem to get through to you. You're starting to wear your pants saggin and worse of all, you're closing your ears to any and everything that your parents are sharing with you for your own benefit.

My mother, who raised me, used to tell me constantly to come home at a certain time, do my homework, stay off that corner, hanging out with guys who don't mean you any good. Like any young man wanting to do what I wanted, I ignored her.

I refused to listen because I thought I had sense. I saw the rappers on television wearing the nice, big gold and platinum chains, nice clothes and shoes and I wanted those things. Since they were always rapping about selling coke and thuggin to get those things, I felt that those were the things to do. Years later, I discovered that I had been deceived! I learned t thuggin wasn't the way to go and I should have taken the cotton out of my ears and listened to my mother. The rappers I used to listen to on BET and my so called friends have never visited me in prison, sent me money, nor wrote me a letter; my mother has though. People whom I have made sacrifices for have abandoned me, leaving me for dead in this place; but again, not my mother.

No one will ever love you like your parents. That's why the Bible teaches us to HONOR our parents; sometimes that's easier said than done. What our parents share with us seems to be a little "out dated." However, in truth brothers, I had to learn that wisdom is never "out dated." If fire was hot yesterday, fire is hot today, and will be tomorrow. So, for real, *for real* – be careful of whom you listen to and seek to emulate. Ask yourself the following questions:

• Who is this rapper or person that I am giving my ear to? And why?

• Is this person I'm giving my ear to real or phony? Wise, or foolish?

• Can I take what this person (rapper, parent, brother, sister, etc.) is placing in my ear and use it to make me a better person in my home and in my community!?

Those are some questions, little brother, that I want you to seriously ask yourself when you are either in the presence of someone trying to influence you to do this or that or when you are in front of that television watching a rapper talk about this or that.

<u>Remember:</u> any information being brought to you, influencing you to be someone other than the image and likeness of god, is negative and unwise and should not be adhered to by you or anyone else who has the ability to exercise common sense!

You can go far if you just use your head and good judgment. Had I done that years ago I wouldn't have to be writing you from a prison cell. A place I hate, but at the same time, a place I now must use to grow and develop. Once I am released, I can be a great benefit and blessing to my family and community; not just another gangstah and thug for them to have to contend with. This is my choice today.

Doing the right thing is my choice because not only is doing the wrong thing out of order and good for nothing, but I don't like being away from my loved ones. They love me so much whereas their birthday wish would be for me to be home with them. I don't like being told when to go to bed and when to get up! I don't like it when my sweetheart comes to visit me in the prison's visitors' room and the correctional officer who oversees the activities tells me not to kiss my girl passionately or touch and rub her soft body. I can't do none of those things when I want to or how I want to because we abide by their rules or suffer the consequences. One of the consequences is spending time in solitary confinement like an animal. Solitary confinement is like a prison inside of a prison. You can only come out for recreation one hour a day. The other twenty-three hours you are locked in a cell as small as the bathroom in your house and the worse part about that is, you got to share that room (cell) with someone else.

That's prison...somewhere you definitely don't want to be or ever come. If you want nice things, and you want to be out of the hood so that you can see better days, don't use drug dealing and thuggin as your first class ticket. If you elect to do so, you may experience a "wolf in sheeps' clothing" or something that may appear to be your pot of jewels. I promise you, on my very own life, that you will discover that all you would have discovered through being a part of the so called "game" is "fool's gold." Fool's gold cannot be cashed in for anything in return that's valuable because it is good for nothing!

Dedicated to my son, Little Kareem, the Prince.

Young Brother, Step Yo' Game Up!

A FEW POINTERS A YOUNG MAN SHOULD CONSIDER BEFORE HE DECIDES TO STEP TO A YOUNG LADY FOR A DATE.

*

I learned so much from my sister when I was in my early teens. She was older than me, and always talking on the phone with her girlfriends. Since she and I were tight, I had access to her bedroom where I could find her on any given day, laid back on her bed talking on the telephone.

Sometimes I would come inside her room not to talk at all with her, but to eavesdrop on her conversations with her girlfriends. Some of the stuff my sister and her girlfriends would talk about would have me laughing up a storm inside.

While a lot of my sister's conversations with her girlfriends would be along the lines of going shopping for the latest name brand outfit, going to the beauty salon, or to some nail parlor, the majority of her conversations would be about "guys" which really would be my main reason for wanting to be nosy and hear whatever it was she had to say.

"Girl, I don't like him at all... he***s*** ugly... he's too aggressive... I don't like a guy who curses all the time..." I overheard my sister say to one of her girlfriends in one conversation.

There would be times my sister would be on the phone for hours just talking about guys, guys, guys! What guys were likeable, and what guys weren't and why.

These nosy moments of eavesdropping served as a

schoolmaster to me in that it helped me to see somewhat of what it might take to secure a young lady's attention, especially if I was in pursuit of a date with some particular young lady.

I tightened up my "swagger," and secured an "A" game demeanor that I would like to now share with all the young brothers who may be finding it hard to score with Sister Beautiful.

Here is what I gathered from my sister and others:

If you want to score with Sister Beautiful, first and foremost come correct in your APPEARANCE. What you look like on the outside says a lot about who you are on the inside. No sister wants to really kick it with a guy who looks "thuggish." That is, unless she's a thug-chick herself. Thug-chicks, as you may know, are chicks who are pretty much chicks who usually attract "dogs" because outside of having a street type mentality, the clothing she usually wears reveal all her meat (if you know what I mean) and nothing gets a dog's tail wagging like meat. This isn't the type of female that a guy who exercises "common sense" would bring home to meet his parents because the first thing your mom is going to say to you later is, "What was that you brought into my house? A woman or a whore?!"

Well, brothers, just like you wouldn't consider dealing with a chick like that (unless you just don't give a you-know-what). No sister, with respect for herself, who she allows herself to associate with, wants a guy who neglects keeping himself well groomed and neatly dressed.

One friend of mine told a guy that although he was handsome, she didn't like the way he wore his pants saggin.

She said that not only was it inappropriate for a guy to show his buttocks because he doesn't buy properly fit jeans, but also, when considering the word "saggin" spelled backwards you get the word "niggas" (someone negative). Plus everything that is associated with bad, ends up with the tag nigga.

She didn't want to be associated with a "nigga" because a "nigga" was someone in her opinion, who went through life carrying on an absent knowledge of his true identity. She said that a man who didn't know himself or care to know himself, could never in truth care to know her. So, she refused baby boy*'s* access to her. Now, this may be something "small" for you, but to Sister Beautiful, it's big.

*

Secondly brothers, if you're hoping to score with Sister Beautiful next to having your appearance intact, come correct in your APPROACH to her. Avoid lines like the one below:

"Yo, whatz up, cu-tieee? Daaamn, girl, your ass is fine! Can a brother holler at you and get them digits?"

Brothers, Sister Beautiful may be humbled by the compliment of you recognizing her cuteness, but the way you did it in that slick, street type of sideways manner was enough to cause her cute face to frown. ***She*** frowned at your approach because it offended her. It offended her because her parents were a great influence in her life and they taught her what to look for when a guy steps to her with interest in scoring a date with her. First of all, her mother gave her a good example to follow by showing her the way. Her mother demonstrated to her how to conduct herself while in public with the eyes of people on her. She taught her daughter how to dress modestly, how to sit in a chair, how she ought to eat at a table, and ***so on***. Besides being her mother and father's daughter, she's GOD'S DAUGHTER, and all of God's daughters are of <u>royal</u> status.

Wherefore, her mother let her know through good example that if a guy refuses, for whatever reason, to recognize the QUEEN in her daughter and fail to show respect in his approach to her along those lines, that a guy is, more than likely, not worthy of her time and attention.

Furthermore, Sister Beautiful learned from her father that a real man is very careful in his approach with a lady. Above all else, she is a lady in every aspect of her demeanor. If he is truly interested in her, the last thing he wants is to blow his golden moment to prove it.

Her father ***also*** taught her that a real man will open doors for her and carry heavy packages. He taught her that a real man will consider his language in her presence, ever quickly to say "excuse me" should a harsh word escape his lips.

She learned from her father, my brother, that a real man will not approach his daughter in a sideways, snake-ish way, but he will approach her in a way that signals respect. No exceptions! Her father taught her also that when it comes to dressing, she should leave some of her body to a man's imagination and that she should let the brother buy the cow, the barn, and the farm before he gets any milk.

So young brother, your approach means a lot. Be straight up with sister. Don't play any games and don't try to act like someone you're not. Take into consideration the way you would want a guy to approach your single mother or your single sister whom you love very dearly. Remember, Sister Beautiful is a lady which means she is not cheap and her time is too valuable to stop what she may be doing to give attention to some "chump" who don't have the slightest idea as to how he should really approach her.

Now, after having your APPEARANCE and APPROACH game strong which for real -for real is enough to hold Sister Beautiful's attention, you really want to make a lasting impression by embracing the right ATTITUDE.

I read a quote by Jesse Jackson once that said,

"It is not your altitude

That determines your ATTITUDE.

It is your ATTITUDE that

Will determine your altitude."

Altitude shows how far up you are from the ground.

If you are willing to gain higher ground with Sister Beautiful, your attitude must be one of humility and patience.

Why "humility?" Humility is far better than "hostility." Plus, it's totally unselfish. Brothers, no young lady wants to be pressured into anything. Understanding this, must lead to you backing up when it comes to certain things with Sister. For instance: Sister Beautiful may allow you to give her a kiss on the lips, because the two of you have been seeing each other more and talking a lot on the phone. However, when you kissed her, you felt an urge to take things a little further. So, you try sliding your hands down sister's jeans only to discover that she stops you and says "no, we can't, I'm not ready."

In spite of her not wanting to go further, you insist that the two of you have nothing to worry about and that the both of you will be fine. Again, she says "no" because she's a virgin, who hasn't finished school and doesn't want to risk getting pregnant. Above all, she doesn't want to risk having sex out of wedlock. She knows that if she allow*s* the two of you to proceed further, she will be going against certain principles and morals her parents instilled in her to guide her by, which makes her resist having sex all the more.

Her saying "no" only makes you angry because after all, you are charged up from a kiss. Besides, all your boys are always bragging on how they ***are*** having mad sex with chicks they deal with. Chicks who don't contest them at all and you want a part of that action of not being contested. So, you forget all about ***how*** Sister Beautiful is a young lady to be respected. Instead, you put more pressure on her, trying your best in the heat of the moment to rush into her panties, but she holds strong and continues to say "no." That's when you push her with your hands away from you, and say, "F**k you then b**ch! I'mma find me another damn girl!"

You walk away without looking back. If you would have looked back, you would have ***seen*** the hurt and disappointment on Sister's face. You would have seen her put her hands together as if about to pray, but instead of praying, tears would be falling from her eyes like a river emptying itself after a heavy rain because you really hurt her. You hurt her by becoming hostile. And, you put a dagger straight through her heart when you no longer recognized her as beautiful. To the contrary, you called her a bitch; a female dog, someone who is supposedly unclean and inhuman. As she ***cries***, brother, she's wondering why you just couldn't be patient and understanding of her situation of not wanting to rush into something that could wait. Now, she doesn't want to have any dealings whatsoever with a guy because she's afraid that he'll hurt her just like you ***did***. So, young brother, whatever you do, be sure to keep the right attitude with Sister Beautiful. Don't get mad and upset at her ***for*** not wanting to degrade herself. Instead, you should be a real man and encourage your queen to remain lady like which would ultimately strengthen your bond with her. The point being, young brother, if your ATTITUDE is genuine and right, Sister Beautiful will trust you and give herself to you when the circumstances are right and not going against her principles and morals. That ***being*** said, brother, you now have the ammo (principles) need***ed***. Now, load up your gun (character) and step your game up!

*

RECAP for your remembrance:

Appearance

What you look like on the outside will let Sister know who you are on the inside. (Apple trees don't produce oranges. A tree is known by its fruit.)

Approach

The manner in which you step toward Sister will determine if she wants to stand before you or step away from you.

Leave the slick, street, thug presentation out of the equation; it will only cause a good Sister to shun you.

Remember, "thugs" are thought of as individuals who sell drugs, carry guns, gangbang, go to prison, and sadly – die young.

In that view, the last thing Sister Beautiful need***s*** in her life is someone who won't be around long enough to enjoy her.

Attitude

Simply put, display good manners in the presence of Sister Beautiful. Be mindful of what you allow to come out of your mouth when addressing her.

If you wouldn't want a male being rude to your grandmother or to your mother, then don't be rude to a daughter of someone else.

"As young black males, we have an obligation and God given duty; to be protectors and providers of our women, children, and community.

But, how can this assignment be accomplished by us when we're constantly locked in chains – primarily for not using our brains except for doing NEGATIVE things?"

Kareem Tomblin

Purpose of Simply Put:

The purpose of writing this book is to encourage my young black brothers who are incarcerated or even on their way to prison – to abandon "thuggin" and committing crime. I also want those who are thinking about breaking the law to stop and think before doing such a thing because prison is not a place you want to be in. I want my young black brothers to know that "cages" are for animals untamed. And that, when we as human beings, who have the potential and power to exercise "common sense", but don't, we become the animals of society who have to be caged; a a harsh ass reality, but one in which we ignorantly bring upon ourselves. Also, one in which you and I can change overnight when we decide to use our heads.

"Circumstances put people in strange places and without the right guidance they falter."

Rose Jackson-Beavers

Only the Strong and Wise Survives

I don't know the amount of time you've been given by the judge to serve in this jungle that you are now an inhabitant of, but if allowed, I would like to share some simple pointers with you from my heart and prison cell, where I have been damn near two decades, 17 years to be exact.

*

Like many "conscious" brothers in the State and Federal Penal System who have "been there" and "done that" as they say, I am concerned about your well being and survival in this jungle where indeed only the STRONG survives. Take it or leave it, but similar to the cold hearted streets and projects most of us who are incarcerated come from, prison is absolutely no place for weak, soft, dumb ass individuals? *(I gotta keep it real with you)*

These places and some of the sick minded individuals within them will quickly and methodically make a "flunky" out of you <u>if</u> you are not on point and strong.

Being on point and strong from what I have come to know and better understand doesn't come from lifting weights or working out extremely hard doing push ups, pull ups, and dips. Neither does such come from carrying knives and grouping up with your "homies" to go for bad...being on point and strong comes in truth from possessing a character that reflects the exercising of good judgment. By that I simply mean: using your head for more than just sporting fly braids, dreads, and fresh fades is what's going to ultimately determine whether you make it out of here or not, alive and well; regardless of your alleged release date! I was told years ago by men who had been incarcerated for longer than I had at that time that if I wanted to survive the madness of being locked away like an animal from my love ones and society, I would have to undeniably BUCKLE MY ASS DOWN, FOCUS LIKE NEVER BEFORE, BECOME LITERATE (Educated), MIND MY OWN DAMN BUSINESS, and CLOSE MY EARS TO ANY/ ALL NEGATIVE THINGS, IGNORANCE, OR STUPIDITY THAT I HAD ALREADY GOTTEN INTO.

You can not enter the penitentiary with a 9mm, or an AK47. You're not entering with your thug associates either. Because nine times out of ten the state or the federal government sent your thug associates to another prison to serve their time. All I had entering the penitentiary to help ease my initial fears was COURAGE which by all means in my view is something you don't need a lot of. But if you don't possess some degree of courage (the ability to stand like a soldier regardless of your fears), you're gonna find yourself doing "hard-time" in whatever prison you're sent to.

“A man is as good as dead if he doesn’t’ learn to wisely use his head.”

Kareem Tomblin

The Real Deal

I have seen young guys enter prison and later get turned into some sick minded muthafuckah's boyfriend. They entered prison a "Maurice" but left a "Mary Ann" because they didn't possess the COURAGE that it takes to stand like a man, they subjected themselves to falling like cowards.

I have also witnessed young brothers who never thought about using drugs like cocaine & heroine on the streets, come into prison and under the heavy weight of the prison sentence that was given to them, they decided that maybe a snort of coke or a needle full of heroine wouldn't hurt. Many of these types of young brothers would eventually become "junkies" in prison. Some would even experience death through overdosing.

In addition, I have seen young brothers turn to alcohol or prison "feel-good-juice" as it is also called, to help drown the reality of having to do time away from loved ones and free society. A lot of these young brothers become so damn addictive to this prison feel-good-juice that they find themselves feening for this shit sometimes more so than they feen for their freedom.

Picking up these type habits, eventually is costly. That's why I said, if you don't possess some degree of COURAGE, you're gonna find yourself doing "hard time"... And in truth, doing hard time only means you're doing time absent of using your head.

However, in spite of me being sent to a damn maximum-security penitentiary and being a little afraid of the damn unknown, I did possess courage. With this courage and a sharp ass mind to pick up on how things go wherever I am, it took no time for me to get caught up in some of the norms of what goes on here in prison. For example: I started hanging out hard with my homeboys on the prison recreation yard, talking about what we did while on the streets and what we fucking had and shit!

I even started smoking a little weed and gambling. I had gotten so side tracked that I literally had forgotten that I was in prison without a high school diploma, without a real sense of WHO I am, other than being a damn thug; and, without getting out of prison anytime soon, unless I got my ass in the law library and started researching my case and how I was railroaded by a crooked ass criminal justice system.

It would take some time, but I would eventually come to my senses. After being sent to solitary confinement after having a prison made weapon (shank) in my possession. I found that the words older individuals had given to me when I first arrived in prison to help with my growth and development, now rang loud within me, as I sat for nearly forty days in solitary confinement. When I was finally released back to the prison's general population, my mind was made up that I was gonna stop "assing" around and do what I needed to do to grow for the better while in this place. It was at that moment, of making that decision that I began to really learn and grow.

"It is not your ALTITUDE that determines

your ATTITUDE.

It is your ATTITUDE that determines

your ALTITUDE."

(Rev. Jesse Jackson)

You Ain't Running Nothing

I had to learn as you will have to learn that, unlike the so-called "free-world," where you are somewhat more privileged to go as you please and do as you want, like: call shots, run things and just plain out be 'the man' – in here you ain't running nothing! Now I'm gonna pause for a moment because I know that you're probably saying within yourself, "What Kareem is feeding me is bull crap because there's a lot an individual can run while here in prison. One can run a gambling table, one can run drugs, wine and cigarettes. Hell, one can even run his mouth and become a snitch like Nicky Barnes and Sammy "the Bull" did in order to score an early release." But Bro., even with those things being thought of and said by you, I still hold strong to my proclamation that in here you ain't running nothing! Those negative thoughts I said you might be thinking about doing, like what I listed above, are things that would make you nothing short of being a CRASH DUMMY!

A Crash Dummy in my view is an Ass. An Ass can be properly defined, virtually in any dictionary, as not only being a donkey, but a STUPID or FOOLISH person. Someone who doesn't think before reacting. Moreover, the fights, stabbings, and even killings in these prisons have either erupted over drugs, gambling, homosexual activity, or over someone trying to just plain out 'get over' on someone they perceived to be overly naive.

These types of things cause problems that you can avoid while exercising common sense that is, if you're truly serious about making a conscious effort to better yourself while your here. I hope that you are, because as I have come to better understand, the very last thing the black community needs in its midst upon your and my release is another "thug" to have to contend with.

"Being on point and strong comes from possessing a character that reflects the exercising of good judgment..."

Kareem. Tomblin

A Number

So far as a result of being in this jungle of incarceration, you and many of us black males here are among other things seen as a NUMBER. Although it is true that we have done many ignorant things, those in high places could care the least to refer to the black males here as NIGGERS. Those in high places have become wise in knowing that the "N-word" which was designed originally to denigrate all black people by those who embraced and promoted the idea of "white supremacy," no longer has a negative effect on us black males today. This makes us want to get up off of our fannies and fight with great power and might for it's abolishment. Consciously speaking, the use of that word should make us black males want to fight for its abolishment because that which is from the forces of evil, designed for our own shame and human debasement could never be used in a manner outside of its original intent.

Yet as young black brothers, in the face of this reality, we are seen and heard using the "N-word" on one another as if it were or could be a positive! Furthermore, to add gasoline to this burning flame of shame and insult towards our people, many of us allow ourselves to be seen and heard calling our beautiful black women "bitches" and "hoes" – as if our black women don't mean a damn thing to us! But the very moment someone calls one of our mothers or sisters one of those derogatory names, we then get mad and wanna severely hurt that person, or worse – kill him/her.

*

Nonetheless, being a NUMBER is how those in high places identify those of us here. So you can get use to hearing the words "count time!" Meaning as far as they are concerned we are nameless because a NUMBER is not a name. A NUMBER is a damn STATISTIC!! Statistics show that one out of three black males in their teens in nearly every major city and state are in trouble; and that, we young black males undisputedly make up the majority of the state and federal penal system's population.

If any of you, my young black brothers, happen to by chance "doubt" our overwhelming presence in these prisons, then conduct the following experiment: go outside to the prison's recreation yard where you know just about everyone in prison hangs out. Look all around you while you're out there, and ask yourself what are the color of the faces I see in my midst? If you are not blind, you will behold a laundry list of black faces. That's right, faces of your very own race. Word is, there are more of us filling these penal institutions than there are of us enrolling in institutions of higher learning (college). And brothers, it don't take a rocket scientist among us to figure out that this is a major problem. Especially when considering that KNOWLEDGE IS POWER!

"A man should know who he is by the knowledge of SELF

that he accumulates.

In the event he is void of such enlightenment, it becomes

more easier for him to go through life undoubtedly being a fake."

Kareem Tomblin

False Characters

The little street name and fame that you and those of us incarcerated may have inherited while being so called big dope boys, stick-up-kids, hitmen, pimps, gangbangers and the like – my advice is that we can now kick that crap to the curb somewhere. Because that wasn't the real us anyway, C'mon, let's just be real about it. That was just some false – buffoonish character that you and those of us here were erroneously influenced to portray in order to survive in a jungle far bigger and worse than the one we are serving time in currently.

Besides, those false – buffoonish-ass characters and reputations don't mean a damn thing to the authorities in high places responsible for securing our stay here. Simply put, regardless of what our so called name and fame was while we're on the streets and in the hood or how BIG we as alleged gangsters and thugs try to portray ourselves to be while here; the truth is, in the eyes of authorities we were no more than a JOKE! You know, something to be laughed at. If they didn't take note of anything else, they certainly took note of the fact that we young black males love to clown around and play which is one of the reasons we had no problem titling our hustle "The Game!"

*

The Game

They say hindsight is 20/20. Well, having learned a little in the past seventeen years of my incarceration about being real, being serious, and above all, being focused – looking back on the matter, I would have to conclude that the title "The Game" is one that I now feel should be renounced by those who still may hold claim to it. Brothers just think about it! Is it a game if you are hustling heroine, powder, crack cocaine and large quantities of marijuana days in and nights out; Coupled with robbing banks, brutally assaulting (and) even killing others to secure and ensure your survival while out there in that world, is this really a game? Even at the expense of not only placing your life in harms way, but also the lives of your love ones. If such activity is seen as being in the arena of "sport and play" then what does that say about your level of seriousness in regards to you hustling illegally? It simply says in my humble opinion that many of us were just out there in that world wasting a lot of precious time – bull-shitting around with this "Game" type of mentality! And brothers it's obvious, what most of us have to show for our alleged criminal involvement; a whole lot of damn "time" to serve! Worse part about it, many of us were "playing" so hard that it ignorantly caused us to mismanage our money which is why when many of us got arrested we didn't even have enough money to afford an attorney to properly represent us in court.

Point being: thuggin' and duckin' and dodging the law as a result of being a part of the criminal way of life to survive, is far from a "game". Slumbering in the mentality of thinking such, is far past the awakening hour.

In any event, now that you are an inhabitant of this jungle, you're not only gonna be viewed as a NUMBER and laughed at for being a JOKE. But you're also gonna be notoriously observed as the BAD GUY! Being observed as the BAD GUY in the authority's eyes means in no uncertain terms that you are a "Con", a "Cheat", a "Loser", a "Thug", a "Mr. Can't Be Trusted", and all of the other negatives. And no matter how close or cool you may happen to become with one of the officers employed by the system, they will not fail to view you (in one way or another) outside of how the "System" taught and trained them to do so. If ever you forget this point of knowledge, you will be not only be flunking the test of "distinction" between them and yourself, but you will also be placing yourself in a position to be wholly disappointed in regards to your perhaps, false expectations of them.

The reality is this! They are the police or the correctional officer as they are also called. The fact they are willing to work in these places brothers, is more than clear and convincing evidence that they are in essence "Co-conspirators" with the iron hand of the State and Federal Government who are definitely responsible for our long – "unjust" prison sentences. I say "unjust" because most of the laws that you and those of us here were sentenced under were specifically designed to bury us young black males which is why we make up over 80 percent of the penal system's population. Congress played a major part in assuring that young African American men received long prison sentences.

In the wake of the Cocaine epidemic of the 1980's, Congress (the law making body of the United States) passed harsh sentencing guidelines and mandatory minimum sentencing laws requiring federal judges in most cases to impose long jail term sentences on anyone convicted of drug trafficking, no matter how small their crime. This law making body of the United States of America was already aware of the fact that most of the Cocaine (powder and crack) was being dealt in the black communities. In fact, it was even discovered that the CIA was directly responsible for placing much of the Cocaine in the black community, starting in California which then spread throughout other areas of the black communities in America. So it can be said that Congress did pass these unjust drug laws with a knowing that the people it would take affect on most would be those of color. What I'm saying on the matter is, if you open your nose, you're gonna smell a shitty diaper! These unjust laws and the system designed to enforce them STINK!

These so called Correctional Officers who lord over us with nothing more than a "key" and the backing of the State and Federal Government are very much aware of our "unjust" long term prison sentences and our presence here. Do they care enough to abandon working for a system that's carrying on this type of injustice? Hell no, they don't care! Not as long as the State and Federal Government are paying them big bucks! Getting the big buck$ are these Officers' chief motive for being here. So, don't be deceived brothers. These so called "Correctional Officers" aren't a bit more here to help you correct from your alleged criminal ways anymore than you and I were out there in that world selling drugs to uplift our community!

To "CORRECT" something means by definition to "make free from fault or mistake"; "to change toward righteousness..." If these so called Correctional Officers and the system they work for were truly focused on helping those of us here correct our wrongs, then why is the recidivism rate so high among us? Over half the inmates who are released RETURN to prison within a two year or less timeframe with the same criminal mind or worst than the one they may have had prior to their first incarceration.

Truth is, when it comes down to you learning anything in prison – especially in a classroom setting, whether it's pursuing your G.E.D., taking a drug treatment class, or any other class that would possibly help you correct your wrongs or help you just to get to the next level educationally, it's your fellow inmates who are the teachers. Yes, it is your fellow "conscious" inmates who teach those among us here who can't read or write - to read and write. And make no mistake about it, it will be your fellow "conscious" inmates who will be the ones to school you on the "dos" and "don'ts" of prison life so that you don't ignorantly get yourself caught up in something that may severely cost you in the long run.

These fellow "conscious" inmate brethren of yours don't get paid the big buck$ that a so called Correctional Officer gets paid, but they love and care for you enough to aid and assist you in your quest for positive growth and development – sometimes staying up one to two o'clock in the morning studying just so that they can be in a better enlightened position to help you. That's why if you don't learn to respect no one else while serving your time, learn to respect your fellow inmates. Respect them all; but especially the ones who help lead you down the right path.

Change has to come from inside and it must be desired by you; otherwise, you will keep falling and stepping on your own feet.

Rose Jackson-Beavers

At Taxpayers Expense

Although it is a tremendous blessing to have your fellow "conscious" inmate brethren in a position to enlighten you so that REHABILITATION can become a reality in your life, it's really the responsibility of the State and Federal Government to bare this burden because they are the ones who get the "funds" to do so. As a matter of fact, that's what the criminal justice system was originally designed for – to assist in every way possible in an alleged criminal's REHABILITATION. But, as time went on, and man's evil schemes began to increase – so did man's greed. That's when those of us who committed crimes – be them petty or major – began to not only be viewed as individuals who should be locked away and helped by the system so that when we return to free society. we would be better equipped to be an asset to our communities and not liabilities. Instead, the alleged criminal began to be viewed as someone who could be imprisoned for a profit; for the most part, at taxpayers' expense!

It cost taxpayers nearly $30,000 to house one prisoner per year. This $30,000 allegedly is used to cover the inmate's food, clothing, medical expenses, etc. Think on this my brother: If the majority of the individuals entering the penal systems of the State and Federal Government are strong, healthy as can be YOUNG BLACK MALES who are undeniably in top notch physical condition, who as a result of this good physical conditioning rarely get sick to the point of becoming chronic medication users, then where is the majority of the taxpayers $30,000 going in this particular area?

Moreover, if those of us here in prison are wearing clothing made by the UNICOR Factory which the inmates operate, getting paid less than nothing for quality work; and, if those of us here in prison are sleeping in a cell no bigger than the average ghetto bathroom – furnished with only two bunks (one for you and the other for your cell-mate), a sink, a small writing table, locker for your personal belongings and a toilet – it's obvious that the taxpayers' dollars are not being spent for us to wear nice name brand clothing or for us to have decent rooms big enough to relax comfortably in. Not that you and those of us here should be living like kings and having it our way. This is prison, make no mistake about it and in truth, we should be made to miss the little luxuries that we enjoyed while in the so called free world. The point that I'm basically trying to get across to you and want you to see is; the taxpayers are being robbed.

This time though, it's not me or you behind the gun. It's important that you grasp this because the taxpayers are our hard working moms, dad, grandparents, etc. It is they who are being used by the system to predominately finance our confinement. If the taxpayers don't ever make some real "noise" about this, then multi-million dollar prisons will continue to be built with their hard earned money to house alleged criminals who are not being rehabilitated by those the taxpayers pay to do this job. This is why brothers, I prefer to not call these so called Correctional Officers – Correctional anything! Instead, I see them as "Collections" Officers and LEECHES; them and the system they work for. Like all LEECHES, they must have something to feed upon or else the leech will die.

*

"... If you don't learn to respect no one else while serving your time, learn to respect your fellow inmates.

Respect them all; but especially the ones who help lead you down the right path..."

Kareem Tomblin

Take it Or Leave It

You can take it or leave it. This unjust system of incarcerating you and those of us here will die overnight if we as intelligent human beings by nature would simply come to our senses and abandon this nonsense of continuing to place ourselves in the arena of committing crime – as if that's all we know to do in order to survive. Surely, there are other ways for us to make a living? But look brother, every time we are released from these Penal Institutions and enter back into society with the mentality of becoming better drug dealers; better bank robbers; better killers; and better CRIMINALS, we are ignorantly giving the State and Federal Government a justifiable reason to lock us away like we're animals for long periods of time! In this regard, the "system" although inherently flawed, is not to be solely blamed for our very own mishaps and errors; SELF is! Self has become one of our worse enemies. The devastating part of it all is most of us don't even seem to give a damn! I say "us" because we are one as a people.

I see many of you, my young black brothers in here for example with 10, 20, 30 years to serve. Many of you are functionally illiterate – unable to read and write past a fourth or fifth grade level – yet, rather than spend the majority of your time in the prison library looking into a book to perhaps further your education, I see you wasting no time to get to the prison recreation yard to play with a "ball" as if someone in authority in these places is gonna offer you a scholarship or some big reward for your ability to dribble and dunk in the manner and style of a Magic Johnson or Michael Jordan!

I'm not hating on you getting your recreation but in truth, what are you RE-CREATING when you recreate? Are you re-creating the same type of clown and buffooning that would cause you to be laughed at as a result of your "priorities" being mixed up? Imagine you without a high school diploma trying to tell your son or daughter to do everything in his/her power to get a high school diploma. Or, worse, imagine your son or daughter coming to visit you with their mom and you are asked by one of them to read a book and they find out that while you are reading, you're having major problems pronouncing words and reading with hindrances. My brother, don't you know that your child is gonna want to know what's up with dad's education level?

Not to mention your child's mom who may be your sweetheart! She's gonna wonder what in the world have you been doing so important in prison with your time that you haven't found the time to educate yourself? Trust me, our family members aren't as dumb and stupid as many of us may think that they are. Our family members are aware of the fact that if a man can't find himself anywhere else or can't educate himself anywhere else, he can do so in a place like prison where there is somewhat of a more separation and solitude from the hustle and bustle of the street way of life that lead us here.

Moreover, unlike those who are free out there in the outside world, those of us incarcerated are free from paying light bills, water bills, rent, and car notes. All we have for real is 'time' to make reformation in our lives a living reality. In truth, none of us here can say that making reformation a reality in our lives isn't possible. By all means, we have Malcolm X as a chief example to the fact that 'bouncing back' from a criminal way of life to a conscious, productive way of life is within our very own grasp.

Before coming to prison, Malcolm was just like many of us incarcerated today. He was in/of the streets. He was known therein as "Big Red" and "Detroit Red." He ran numbers, sold liquor and dealt drugs. After entering prison on charges of grand larceny and breaking and entering, Malcolm was introduced to the teachings of the Nation of Islam as taught by its leader the Honorable Elijah Muhummad. The Honorable Elijah Muhummad taught Malcolm among other things, the knowledge of God and the knowledge of Self. Most importantly, the knowledge of God and the Knowledge of Self is what had been taken away from black people as a result of our fore parents having been enslaved by the white slave master who was so evil and cruel that he didn't even permit our fore parents to pick up a book to learn.

After years and years of this type of cruelty, our black people had nowhere else to go but down. In this downward spiral, many of our people fell into lifestyles of acting beyond and beneath our true and original selves. Malcolm was not an exception. Through embracing the teachings of the Honorable Elijah Muhummad, he found his opportunity to bounce back; and bounced back he did! He stopped using drugs; he stopped smoking cigarettes, and he stopped using foul, filthy language because the Honorable Elijah Muhummad taught him that those things keep our mind and body unclean. An unclean mind and body could never be the true temple of God.

Malcolm sharpened his mind by also studying the dictionary, Holy Koran, Holy Bible, and countless other books; all of which aided this change. Malcolm's change was so real and genuine that when he was finally released from prison, he never came back for doing anything criminal.

*

“The ultimate measure of a man is not where he stands in moments of comfort and convenience, but where he stands at times of challenge and controversy.”

Martin Luther King

Bouncing Back Is An Option

I want to say unto you my young black brothers incarcerated that, regardless of what you have done or how much time you have been given by the judge representing the State or Federal Government, "bouncing back is an option!" The greatest way of accomplishing this goal in my humble opinion is with God. The Holy Bible teaches that 'with God, all things are possible!" (Luke 1:37)

Not even Malcolm X, with all of the knowledge that he had accumulated while in prison, could have accomplished all that he did without submitting himself to God. It's our very nature to submit to God because it was in God's Image and likeness that all of us human beings were made. Read Genesis 1:26. If we, as human beings, were made in the image and likeness of God, that makes us the same as God is – just on a "lower level." Which is why Jesus, The Messiah taught in the Gospels "ye are all gods..." (John 10:34).

We, as humans, being "gods" is not Jesus teaching us "Religion," it's him teaching us our very own nature.

Brother's it is our very own nature as "gods' to be supreme "righteous" thinkers just as our Creator and God is. I say "righteous" because it's far from God to do anything "wrong" which is why wrongdoing should be far from our way of life. Snatching some old lady's purse is wrong; having children and not taking care of them as a Man should, is wrong; ANYTHING that would cause you or me to go against our very on nature of "righteousness" is wrong and should not be adhered to by any of us who have the ability to exercise "Common Sense." Exercising "Common Sense" must become our greatest practice if "bouncing back is gonna become a reality in our lives. You and I, while here in prison, can take all the classes being offered by the educational department; we can equally and faithfully attend every church service; as well as mosques meetings, but if we don't exercise common sense in the areas of our lives where we seem to be so trouble proned, we're gonna always find ourselves stuck in the mud of low living and shame.

Common sense essentially says unto us, "IF FIRE IS HOT, DON'T TOUCH IT!" Don't touch it because fire has the power to disfigure whatever is laid upon it. So it is when you and I lay ourselves on thuggishness and wrong doings, our lives become disfigured; disfigured for example, with us having to spend some of our best damn years behind "steel doors" and "concrete walls"!

Common sense also says unto us, if you don't want others hurting or harming you, then you must not go out of your way to hurt or harm others. Do unto others as you would have them do unto you.

This is what many would call the GOLDEN RULE. One thing I've learned about gold from mainly wearing a lot of it when I was out in the streets thuggin is, gold is one of the most valuable jewels on the planet earth. People from damn near all over the world who can afford a piece will purchase it because of its value. Likewise, you and I can become valuable when we begin to exercise common sense and learn to do unto others what we would want others to do unto us. Don't get me wrong though, this won't be easy, especially not in a world where fighting fire with fire is damn near the norm. But with God, all things are possible, even you and I, renouncing being thugs for life. The choice is ours. Simply put!

"I leave you with faith. Faith is the first factor in a life devoted to services. With it, nothing is impossible.

Faith in God is the greatest power, but great, too, is faith in oneself."

Mary McLeod Bethune

Enlighten Thinkers

The black community is in desperate need of "enlighten thinkers" and "activists" both young and old, who possesses the wisdom and power to "bless" and not further "curse" our community. By all means, our black communities are cursed enough. Cursed with poverty and cursed with HIV/AIDS. Did you know black woman leads the nation among other races of women in HIV/AIDS? (Think over that). In addition, high blood pressure and diabetes are destroying our community, mainly because our people refuse to exercise and eat the proper food that causes the body to be of good health and not that of bad health.

Our black communities in various cities and states are cursed with young black brothers hanging out on street corners hustling drugs and being a part of gangs that do nothing but negative sh** in the community. What's more disturbing is how cursed our community is with single black female mothers raising our children "alone" because the "male" who slept in the bed with her and got her pregnant, has utterly abandoned his fatherly responsibilities to his child. How we, black men abandon our responsibilities as it relates to being there and taking care of our children and not loving them enough, remains a mystery to me. There is no way I could dress a BENZ up over dressing my "babies" with a secured future.

Simply Put, there is no way our community can continue to survive with the above mentioned negatives, existing within it's midst anymore than a human body can continue its health and strength with a chronic illness constantly attacking it with the absence of proper medication to counter attack it.

One last thing I would like to share with you. If you are serious about not only putting forth the effort to change your life, but also getting out of prison as early as possible, don't go "rat" on somebody to do so. These Penal Institutions are full of rats. Many of them have lied on others just to secure early releases. That's wrong and "karma" will catch up to individuals who do that. My advice to you is get out of prison the right way. Go over to the prison Law Library and begin researching your case. What you don't know, don't be ashamed to ask your fellow convicts who are very knowledgeable in the legal field. Many of them are dying to help you. However, you must be willing to "help yourself" as well. Since the federal government has a 98 percent conviction rate as a result of individuals taking "plea bargains." Here are a few documents you will need to contest the validity of a guilty plea:

1. Police reports; DEA 6 reports; FBI reports; ATF reports (whatever the case may be)

2. Indictment or Information (whichever the case may be)

3. Docket Entry Sheet; All motions

4. Motion to Suppress; Search warrant; Arrest warrants; Affidavits used to obtain the search warrant

5. Suppression hearing transcripts

6. Guilty Plea Transcripts

7. Letters from your attorney advising you of the conditions or terms of your plea

8. Presentence Report (due to BOP policy, you have to go to your Case Manager to review your PSI report)

9. Objections to Presentence Report

10. Sentencing Transcripts, Judgment and Commitment Order, and Notice of Appeal

If you are in the 2 percent category who went to trial, you will need the documents stated below to contest your conviction and sentence:

1. All investigative reports whether Police reports' ATF reports; DEA & reports; FBI reports (whatever the case maybe)

2. Search Warrants, Arrest Warrant, and Affidavits used to obtain said warrants

3. Indictment of information (whichever the case may be)

4. Docket Entry Sheet

5. Motion to Suppress and any other pretrial motions (if possible)

6. Suppression and motion hearing transcript (if possible)

7. Proposed jury instructions by the defense, (if any)

8. Trial transcripts, including jury selections' opening arguments, trial motion hearing during the course of the trial, closing arguments and sentencing

9. Jury Instructions charged

10. Verdict forms requested and verdict forms actually

used

11. Any and all motions for new hearing on motion for new trial, judgment of acquittal, or arrest of judgment

12. Presentence Report and Objections to PSI report

13. Sentencing Transcripts,Judgment and commitment order

14. Notice of Appeal

15. Appellant and Apelles briefs (if any)

All of the information I have listed above are things that my fellow convicts taught me while attending their law classes. I hope and pray that this information will be of a help to you as it was to me.

So Cold/So Cruel

This is a mean and evil world; so cold, so cruel. I mean, just look. Why is there so little love shown toward one another on humanity's part? Why are there so many of us human beings mobilizing on life's highway with broken hearts? Why are there so many starving children in a world full of food and wealth? And let us consider Africa and how it's inhabitants are dying from HIV/AIDS, crippling it's peoples' health. Let us take a hard look at the Iraqis and the American troops fighting to their death over in the Middle East.

Former President George W. Bush said, "It's A War on Terror." If that be the naked truth, then he should've been like Michael Jackson and started with the man in the mirror! How could a former President send U.S. Troops off to war for a cause rooted deeply in lies? No weapons of "Mass Destruction" were ever found, yet thousands have had to die. I say enough is enough and it's way past time to let the truth be made known, and indict Bush and his former administration for war crimes!

Further more, another injustice is blazing like a gasoline fire; it's not hard to tell. America has the highest incarceration rate in the world with over 2.4 million locked away in jail cells!

This is a titanic problem, one in which someone has got to take a stance. How can any Judge sentence a man to "life" for selling cocaine and not offer him/her a second chance?

Most of those incarcerated are young black males. Individuals who grew up very poor and felt they had to make a few crack sells to survive. Moreover, the U.S. eonomy is tremendously down. Jobs are scarce and we all can clearly see from the "Jena 6" incident that racism and hatred still exist. This is a mean and evil world; so cold and so cruel. I wonder if your eyes are open out there. If so, what are you going to do?

We can move mountains with God, faith, determination, and persistence. Yes we can!

Rose Jackson-Beavers

YES WE CAN!

(A message to my brothers in the streets "thuggin")

I wanna share something that ought to inspire you to look past the "haters" and their "drama". It's what I believe every thug, as I was, should know about Barack Obama. This brother is real. This brother is true. And as a black man living in America, he has suffered some of the same discriminations from others as you and me. He has been called a "nigger" and has been told that he would never amount to much. But with hard work, education, and courage, he has caused many mouths to hush. As a highly intelligent Lawyer and Senator, for the poor and needy he fought like heck, guided by God – Yes! Without compromise, he is assisted by his beautiful black Queen, Michelle.

But being Senator wasn't enough, there were other dreams he had that were also great. Dreams like becoming the President of the United States. When he announced to the world that he would seek the Presidential Office of a Nation rooted deeply in racism and hate, some became afraid of his life, and said, "Barack, you're making a mistake." Barack blocked out those voices of fear and put his fate in God's hands. He knew that with God, he was more than a conqueror, so he proclaimed the words, YES WE CAN! With this type of faith and determination, an alleged "underdog" black man is now the COMMANDER and CHIEF of our nation.

I believe he is a man "heaven sent." I believe he is someone we all can trust. I also believe that CHANGE can come in America, but like he said, "It's gonna take ALL OF US".

ALL OF US include the thugs. Brothers we have got to put away our guns and drugs to help make change a reality. We can do this if we take courage and renounce embracing the devil's mentality. Besides, what has thug life gotten us – except prison or death? Think about it, if we continue this foolishness, very few of us black males will be left; now that would be a shame. No, really it would be a crime for us to go continuously through life wasting precious time.

We must gain knowledge, get off the corners and enroll in college. Take care of our CHILDREN, that's the responsibility of a father. We must stop disrespecting our Queens, calling them "bitches" and "hoes." How can a black woman be those names when her man is on his post? When her man is on his post and doing the right thing, sister will have no other choice but to do right and aid her king. Think about it, the odds may be against us because we're black and have thugged a bit, with the right guidance from above, we can do like Barack and prove our critics wrong. In truth, only God can determine ones' fate; it's truly in His hands and divine plan. However brothers, let's do everything in our power with the mind that God gave each one of us, and move from "thug" to "thinker."

It's possible. Therefore, YES WE CAN!

Simply Put

Simply Put, if you don't want to end up in a jail cell without your freedom, there are several things you can do:

- Stay out of trouble
- Listen
- Educate yourself and stay in school
- Follow your own path
- Surround yourself with people who want things legally
- Stay away from drugs
- Remember fast money does not last
- Once you get locked up, it's extremely difficult to get out
- Love yourself because when you do, it's hard for people to talk you into doing something that will hurt
- If by chance you do get in trouble and end up in jail, use this opportunity to think, study, and learn to become a better you.
- Finally seek God, not glitter!

"Circumstances put people in strange places and without the right guidance, they falter."

Rose Jackson-Beavers

More about the Author

"To know me, is to hear me.

To hear me, is to feel me.

To feel me, is to understand that

I am a man. And no man is perfected

before his appointed time."

(Kareem)

"Moreover, I saw under the sun: In the place of Judgment, (Courthouses), wickedness was there..."

(Ecclesiastes 3:16)

Interview of Kareem Tomblin

INTRODUCTION

The Authorities for the Government of the Western District of North Carolina/Charlotte Division claimed that I, and my alleged co-conspirators, conspired together to commit robberies of known drug dealers, conducted numerous home invasions, and was responsible for various drug related homicides. The Government claimed that all of these unlawful acts were done by me and my co-conspirators in the name of maintaining and protecting the interest of "THE WEST CHARLOTTE POSSE!"

Whether we were in fact the notorious organized street gang of young black males said to have been so menacing that nearly every weapon in the federal arsenal was used to remove us from the streets, is a question that I, Kareem, the youngest alleged member of the West Charlotte Posse will address truthfully. I will also address the primary reason I, as a youngster at that time in my life, decided to embrace the "street way" of doing things, and more.

This interview was conducted by a very special friend of mine whom I went to school with, prior to me embracing the streets. I will keep her identity in the closet, I will say, that while working for the B.O.P. (Federal Bureau of Prisons), she and I crossed paths. This interview resulted from that.

This very special sister-friend of mine decided that it would be a good idea to bring this interview to you, the reader, because as many of you are much aware, everything that one hears in the news media, or read in the newspapers is not always correct. The West Charlotte Posse case was widely exposed in the news media and newspapers back in 1992 at the time of our arrest and detention. Much of this exposure was tainted by reporters whose job is to come up with headline stories that boaster the sells of their newspapers, etc. So this interview is an opportunity for you, dear reader, to get it straight from the horses' mouth. It's also an opportunity for the "haters" to put away their judgmental attitude; like this certain deputy who was working in the county jail at the time of my court proceedings. This guy screamed out, "I hope you and the rest of your co-conspirators get the death penalty!"

This individual didn't at all know the facts or truths surrounding me and my co-conspirators' case. This guy was simply under a bad dose of misinformation fed to him by the news media.

I stated that to state this: chances are, if you're not getting what you need to know from a "reliable" source, then you may be getting as Brother Malcolm X would say, "Hoodwinked" or "bamboozled!"

JUST BEING TRUTHFUL

(THE INTERVIEW)

QUESTIONS BY: Sister-Friend
ANSWERS BY: Kareem
PLACE: Somewhere in the FEDS

S.F.: "Hey handsome, how have you been doing?"

Kareem: "I'm maintaining, you know, doing what I gotta do under the circumstances to survive, but all is well."

S.F.: "Well, you're looking good as always."

Kareem: "Thank you, sister."

S.F.: "I want you to know that I had every intention of doing this sooner, but something came up and I had to take a trip to Atlanta on some business."

Kareem: "You're always going somewhere on business."

S.F.: "Yeah, and I apologize, because you and I had already set a day for this project and I was really looking forward to just getting it on. There's just so much I would like to inquire of you."

Kareem: "Well, baby girl, let's get to it because time is of essence, plus I have been wanting to do this since we reconnected."

S.F.: "Okay then Mr. Tomblin, let me begin by..."

Kareem: Let you begin by addressing me by my first name,

Kareem, and not by my last name Tomblin. I shared with you some letters ago, I try not to acknowledge that name at all."

S.E.: "I remember you sharing that with me once, but you never gave unto me an explanation as to why you chose to not acknowledge it. What's wrong with Tomblin?"

Kareem: "I choose not to acknowledge it because in my opinion, Tomblin is a name placed upon my fore-parents without their permission or consent. Even if this was not so, I still would seek to renounce it just the same because Tomblin sounds too much like "tumbling" which comes from the root word "tumble" meaning "to fall!" To fall implies failure---so, calling me Tomblin is like calling me a failure!"

SE: "Boy, you're something. So, who placed this name on your fore-parents? You know I'm curious."

Kareem: "The white slave master!"

S.E.: "Oh, ok, as in the days of slavery. Well, does "Kareem" carry any meaning?"

Kareem: "Yes it does, and I'm glad that my father blessed me with that name. It's a name of Arabic origin meaning "Respectful" or "Honorable."

S.E.: "That's good. Do you consider yourself "Respectful," or "Honorable?"

Kareem: "I try to be respectful...to all, regardless of who you are or what type of lifestyle that one chooses to be involved in. I've honestly been like that all of my life, even when I was thuggin and shit."

S.E.: "A lot of guys, Kareem, come to prison and convert to

Islam and I remember you telling me one time that a lot of guys that you meet sometimes mistake you for being Islamic or a Muslim because of your name...are you in fact Muslim?"

Kareem: "No, sister, I am not a Muslim, although as you stated, a lot of people whom I have encountered do assume I am based upon the fact that my name is Islamic."

S.F.: "What do you consider yourself Spiritually?"

Kareem: "A human being!" which by all means is a spiritual title. How could it not be when the first individuals, according to the Holy Bible, were created in the image and likeness of God whom Jesus taught was a "Spirit!" (See Genesis 1:26 and John 4:24). Now, God being a "Spirit" doesn't mean that God is a spook or something untouchable! God being a "Spirit" just means that God is a "Character" of supreme intelligence unmatched by any in the universe. He created human beings to reflect His "Character" of supreme intelligence which is why we can create things like telephones and televisions, etc. Being human also means that we have the ability to exercise common sense! Don't get me wrong now sister, I attend church, fast, and make prayers, but I've been incarcerated seventeen years of my life and have found that the greatest spiritual "gift" that the Creator gave unto us to guide by is "common sense!" It's a gift within all of us if only we but took the time out to heed its wisdom. Sister, this is so serious because common sense essentially says: "If fire is hot, don't touch it!" If you don't want others hurting or harming you, then you must not go out of your way to hurt or harm others!" So, in answering your question: A human being is what I consider myself to be spiritually."

S.F: "I agree with your insight on that matter, but Kareem, I just can't seem to get over the fact that you've been incarcerated 17 years! My gosh, it just doesn't seem like it's been that long!"

Kareem: "It's been that long; I was 17 years old at the time of my arrest and detention. I am nearing 35 years old."

S.F.: "You were only a kid!"

Kareem: "The government used the word "juvenile!" but I guess William Shakespeare once stated: "A rose by any other name would be just as sweet!"

S.F.: "Yeah, if you were a flower, but you're a human being, as you've just shared and it pains my heart when I think of you being in a place like this which I personally think is designed for animals; something you're not! I mean, we went to school together and everything. I used to let you copy my homework and didn't mind at all because you were always nice. Plus, you used to rock the crowd with your little rap group that was called um...um..., what was it called?"

Kareem: "It was called B.F.B. That is the only little hint that I'm giving you."

S.F.: "Yeah, B.F.B., Be Fresh Boys! Boy, I must admit, I had the biggest crush on you back in those days."

Kareem: "You never showed it!"

S.F.: "Like you would have paid me any attention if I would have.... H-E-L-L-O!"

Kareem: "It wasn't like I was "Tupac" or any other big rap super star!"

S.F.: "But you and I both know that in our little school, you were just as popular!"

Kareem: "You know how to make a brother feel good, I know that!"

S.F: "Okay, Mr. I- know- how- to- make- a- brother- feel- good! Anyway, I want to eventually get into this "West Charlotte Posse" stuff, but first Kareem, curiosity gets the best of me in wanting to know what influenced you as a young man to involve yourself with the criminal activities of the streets? As I alluded to previously, you were a rapper with a group that appeared to have had all the necessary ingredients of becoming famous, what happened? I mean, where did things go wrong?"

Kareem: "It's a long story sister, but in truth, poverty was at the heart of my decision to do what I felt necessary to do in the days of my involvement in/with the streets. Neither fame nor fortune was my motive, but simply just wanting to be in a position to help my mother in her quest to feed and provide for our family. It was six of us, four boys and two girls and I got tired of seeing her struggle day in and night out alone; so circumstances would have it. I found my way into the streets. I didn't want to, but at age 14 years old, I was considered too young to get a legitimate job at Burger King or McDonald's. The law in N.C. was that you had to be 16 years old and at least, if you were 15 years old, you probably could get away with working a summer job. Since I was, by law, under-aged, my attention was directed towards the streets. Not only was it a way for me to get fast cash, but also a life that very few live to escape from in one piece! I started hustling drugs, but to be completely honest and truthful with you sister, I never considered myself a drug dealer. I'm not saying that I wasn't good at it because I am damn good at hustling that shit, but my reputation came as result of me robbing these type individuals."

S.F.: "But why would you target these individuals to rob?"

Kareem: "Mainly because in my mind I somewhat had a

dislike for them, but it wasn't personal. It was all about how they would parade themselves around in the hood amongst the poor in their big shiny Cadillac's, expensive jewelry, nice clothes, and shoes, etc., like they were the untouchable "kings of the hill!" So, instead of me sticking up a mom and pops' type store or any other legitimate place of business, I made the dope boys my target."

S.F.: "Were you ever afraid of losing your life because I'm sure that sticking up these types of individuals can be a bit dangerous."

Kareem: "Sure, doing such is a bit dangerous as you just put it and there were times when I was afraid, but one thing about being in and out of the streets, you quickly learn to conquer your fears; in the event you don't, you may not last. Besides, when my father rolled out, leaving my mother, my siblings, and me to fend for ourselves, I died at that moment. My life as a youngster was officially over!"

S.F.: "I can feel you on that, Kareem, because hell, I grew up without my father being present as well. That shit hurts too."

Kareem: "It does hurt because I firmly believe that had he stuck it out, like a real man, I wouldn't be in prison today.

S.F.: "You haven't spoken with your father since you've been incarcerated?"

Kareem: "It's funny you asked that because somehow when I was behind the wall (Penitentiary), he and I managed to hook up. I don't know how I actually got his address, probably from my grandmother, his mother, whom I call from time to time. I wrote him concerning how I felt at the time about us and our family. Well, he wrote back apologizing and what not and of course, I forgave him about seven months afterwards. He passed away from a serious liver illness. I took it extremely hard because he and I were in the process of rebuilding our relationship."

S.F.: "I can imagine, but at least the two of you got the chance to reconcile before he passed."

Kareem: "Yes, and I'm thankful unto God for that. Now, a brother can move on."

S.F: "Let's shift gears a little and talk about the "West Charlotte Posse" that you were alleged by the Government to not only have been a member, but an active participant, ranking as a Lieutenant under Adrian Lamont Davis, the alleged ring leader! The legal paper work that you sent to me for my review in no uncertain term declares, according to investigative reports, filed by the United States Bureau of Alcohol, Tobacco and Firearms (BARF), and trial testimony, that during December 1991, continuing through September 1992, Mr. Davis and co-defendants collectively known as "The Posse," conspired together to possess and distribute quantities of cocaine base heroine, in the Charlotte, North Carolina area. The members of this organization possessed and used firearms to: steal illegal drugs from rival drug dealers which they would then resell; steal money from rival drug dealers which they would use to support "The Posse" operations; assault and kill rival drug dealers; protect the organization's drugs and money; and kidnap individuals to extort illegal drugs and money from other drug dealers. "The Posse" organization was also referred to by its members as "N.B.C." which reportedly stood for "NIGGAS BEING CRUCIAL!" The term Niggas NIGGAS was said to stand for NEVER IGNORANT GETTING GOALS ACCOMPLISHED. Kareem, there was a laundry list of allegations against you guys and the list goes on, but how much of what the Government alleged you guys did is actually and factually true?"

Kareem: "Very little of this garbage is true which is why I am so glad you're questioning me concerning the matter. This Government, all it does is lie, lie, lie, and lie! You know, as in the case of there being weapons of mass destruction over there in Iraq, nothing has been found over there to prove those allegations. Yet, United States troops are over there getting shot and killed by thousands as a result of this misleading information. Adrian Lamont Davis, Donald (D-Nice) Thomas, Michael (Reddy Mike) Rozelle, myself (Kareem Abdul Tomblin, a.k.a. "Gucci"), and others said to have been connected to this "posse" case were given vey long stretches of time to do in this federal system with no chances of parole, as a result of this Government (FBI, BATF, Prosecuting Attorneys, etc,.) making us out to be this notorious organized street gang with "mafia type structure!" I admit that drug dealers were robbed by me and others which at times, things got violently taken to the next level."

S.F.: "By that you mean?"

Kareem: "By that I mean, blood was shed!"

S.F.: "As in the "Clyde Drive" incident where one Jamaican got his face nearly blown off and where another Jamaican, who also was a big heroin dealer you guys were robbing, was severely shot and paralyzed for life."

Kareem: "Yeah, and I know that such an incident as the one you just described is a horrible act, but sister, we're talking about the underworld of the streets where it's, as I prefer to put it "winter cold!" You can't get caught half-steppin' because in that criminal life, anything goes! Those who enter into it have to do with some degree of knowledge of the fact that if it ever goes down, somebody may not make it back home. It's nothing short of a 'war-zone.' As you know, in every war there are casualties, but as far as this "posse" thing is concerned, we all sold drugs and stuff like that, but we weren't at all an 'organization!' We were in truth, a bunch of loose-knit black males, 16-25 years old, me being the youngest, who were by all means misguided and immature. Although the Government initiated its prosecution of me as a juvenile, the truth of the matter is, mentally, we all were juveniles! However, the Governmental authorities, in my very firm opinion, had a bigger agenda than just wanting to clean up streets predominately inhabited by 'blacks!' You and I both know that they don't give a shit about us enough to do that!"

S.F.: "So, you believe that there was a hidden agenda on the behalf of the Governmental authorities for aggressively prosecuting you and your conspirators as they did?"

Kareem: "Certainly, because prior to the Governmental authorities prosecuting us, they came down hard on some other "young black males" and falsely labeled them as "The Cecil Jackson Gang!" The alleged ring leader received life in the federal system and many of his co-conspirators received very lengthy prison terms as well; many of whom may never get out! Anyway, nearly two years after those guys were arrested and convicted, another group of young black males were arrested for selling drugs and committing acts of violence and what do you know, "The Feds" come along and snatch the case for the "State" who originally assumed jurisdiction and labeled my co-conspirators and me "The West Charlotte Posse!" As a result of this fraud, for the very first time in the history of the western district of Charlotte, NC, the Anti-Racketeering Statute was applied to us, aggressively being prosecuted! The Government never could have used the statute against us concerning gang activity if the Government doesn't first somehow establish that we were in fact a "gang!" So, their task was to first and foremost make us out to be an organized, violent street gang!"

S.F.: "But why would the Government authorities target you guys to do this?"

Kareem: "Sister, because being "young, black, and violent" is a big business for them and in 1992, my co-conspirators and I fit that description. All the Government did was cash in on through their deceptive intelligence."

S.F.: "Damn!"

Kareem: "That's right, it's a known fact among State and Government officials that, the tougher the law enforcement is on crime, the bigger and better their chances are of being promoted to a higher ranking position! In addition, I have even discovered since I've been incarcerated and according to Federal Code (title 5 4501-2-3-4), prosecutors and judges are allowed bonuses ranging from $10,000 to $25,000 for their meritorious service. Their meritorious service is locking up young black males and giving them outrageous time! The time given to us 'federal prisoners' doesn't carry the possibility of parole! Meaning, 85 percent of our time has to be served before we can ever be released."

S.F.: "Yeah, but didn't you guys have good trial attorneys to contest what the Government was alleging because we're talking about some very serious charges here that you guys were facing!"

Kareem: "It was indeed a very critical moment for us and yes, we all had attorneys, but guess what? The attorneys that we had were court appointed attorneys! A court appointed attorney is an attorney given to you by the court when you are unable to afford one of your own."

S.F.: "Wait one minute, Kareem, you mean to tell me that out of all cocaine and heroin the Government alleged you and your co-conspirators sold, as well as, all of the money you guys were taking from other drug dealers to finance the Posse's operations that not one of you could afford to hire a decent attorney to represent you guys' best interest in court?"

Kareem: "Now are you starting to see the lie perpetrated upon us by this Government? I shared with you earlier that we were no more than a bunch of misguided black males doing what we felt necessary to survive out there in that jungle called "The World!" However, when all was said and done, my alleged co-conspirators and I were added to this Government's 98 percent conviction rate. Again, this goes back to not having skilled trial attorneys with our best interest at heart. All these court appointed attorneys try and get you to do is become a Government 'snitch!' If you're not assisting the Government, it's an uphill battle for you!"

S.F.: "Are you're appealing your conviction and sentence?"

Kareem: "Certainly! I refuse to sit back idly and not voice what I believe to be right and exact in my quest to regain my freedom. In 1996, Former President William Jefferson Clinton signed into law the Anti-Terrorist Bill which among other things, put a time limitation on all petitions filed in Court; this has made it extremely difficult for many of us incarcerated to get out! After all, none of us are professional attorneys and very few of us incarcerated go over to the law library to study the law and how it applies to our case. By the time we do learn of it (the law), the one year time lapse has been expired and you're stuck in this place without ever getting the opportunity to be heard in court because they're gonna deem you "time barred!" Such is the hurdle for me at the moment, but with the divine intervention of the Creator, I'll eventually prevail because I got documented proof that I was transferred from juvenile to adult status illegally, so, it's just a matter of time!"

S.F.: "What about your other co-conspirators; are they appealing their conviction and sentence?"

Kareem: "If they are not, stupid they are, but we don't keep in touch as much as we should. I do, however, get a message from several of them every now and then."

S.F.: "What is your relationship with Adrian Davis and why was he singled out by the Government as the "ring leader" of this so-called gang you guys were made out to be?"

Kareem: "Adrian Davis is considered by me to not only be my brother in this fight, to destroy the lies that our case and conviction was predicated upon, but he is also a soldier! I still have no idea though as to why the Government picked him out to be the notorious ring leader of this 'West Charlotte Posse' but, such in my opinion, is a gigantic act of 'fraud' on behalf of the Governmental authorities and was the very reason he received the most undeserved time among those of us on this case. I've never ever seen Adrian Davis shoot or kill anyone! Neither have I ever heard of him giving any of us whom he associated with any type of orders to kill. Besides, not one of us associated with this case was ever in a position to order anything. We had our own minds and no one was telling any of us to do something that we didn't already have in mind. To the contrary, the prosecuting attorneys claim that Adrian Davis was such a ruthless gang leader that all he had to do was utter "smoke 'em" and members of the Posse would kill. However, as I have stated, nothing could have been further from the truth."

S.F.: "I just hope that he is fighting like crazy to get that time back that he has because the Government loaded him up!

Kareem: "And so do I, but this Government is most vicious! They will do anything and everything to keep you behind bars;

especially if you're not cooperating with them, sister."

S.F.: "Man, that's cold as a muthafuckah! And I do mean that literally, Kareem."

Kareem: "Naw, baby girl, that's more than "cold." That's the **devil** personified through the wickedness of the United States Government! How can you take a young man in his late teens or early twenties and give him 20, 30, 40 years in prison or give him a life sentence based on bullshit, if you are not evil? Since I've been incarcerated, I haven't seen one white male with the type of time given to us black males. You mean to tell me blacks are the only ones committing crime?"

S.F.: "Man, I feel you on that shit. The Government got all of my black bruthas on lock up; it's racist and it's wrong! It's got to change."

Kareem: "It will change. Nothing stays the same forever. Nothing, sister."

S.F.: "Not changing the subject, but where would you be if you hadn't come to prison?"

Kareem: "I probably would have gotten killed or something because it's no secret, I was off the chain, so much so that I personally prayed for God to deliver me from the life that I was living. This is how I know that prayer changes things, especially when you really mean it from your heart. Not long after I prayed the prayer, I got locked up! This experience was most definitely a must and to be completely honest with you, I wouldn't exchange it for nothing in this world! The only thing I would change is experiencing injustice."

S.F.: "Well, it's obvious that you have undergone a change and I'm sure that all who knew you prior to you experiencing incarceration, would bare me witness, it's all in your mannerism, talk, and demeanor! The things you say, even when you write to me, are things that make me think and wanna do better. Tell me, who influenced you to be the man that you are becoming today?"

Kareem: "I would have to say, firstly, my personal relationship with Christ and His teachings which are essentially designed to bring us to our senses in hopes of us doing the right thing by our Creator and fellowman. Secondly, I must say Malcolm X and his autobiography influenced me a great deal to consider changing my life. It's sort of strange because since I was the youngest on this 'West Charlotte Posse' case, the Government placed me in a juvenile federal facility in Asheville, NC where the director there (who is similar to a warden in a prison), personally came to my room one day and just handed me a book and before I could say anything, he said to me, "I brought this for you, take your time and read it!" I saw that it was the autobiography of Malcolm X and I replied humbly with the words, "Thank you sir, I appreciate this!" He then walked away with just a few last words, "Just be sure to read it." "Okay," I nodded my head backward and forward, "Yes sir, I will." I did with gladness, in doing so, I discovered a man who was a 'thug' to say the least, who found himself incarcerated as a result. However, while incarcerated, Malcolm underwent a transformation after hearing and receiving knowledge that possessed the power to break the chain of ignorance and misguidance over him which had so easily caused him to be the thug that he was, prior to this encounter. He stopped playing sports replacing his life of stupidity with a life in search of God and self and what he could do to make life for his people better, as well as humanity in general. Today, as a result of Malcolm X coming to his senses, getting out of prison, doing the right thing, he is a household name in America and around the world! So, I felt that if he could change, then so could I. He has been a role model and very powerful influence on my growth and development since."

S.F.: "Do you believe that you have a purpose in this life?"

Kareem: "Of course sister, we all do!"

S.F.: "And what might yours be? Or, do you know?"

Kareem: "I believe that my purpose in this life is to help destroy the works of ignorance in/and among my generation and the next. In truth, we are in grave trouble! This is because we don't love and respect the ways of God as we should, neither do we pursue 'education' with a passion as we should, this is most critical, especially among us so called African Americans. I'm always reminded of the horrible years (hundreds of them), that our ancestors spent being enslaved by the white slave master who forbid them to read or even think about wanting to educate themselves. If our ancestors were even caught with a book in their possession, they would be brutally beaten beyond what you or I could ever imagine today. So, education must be aggressively pursued by African Americans with a knowing that 'knowledge is power!' Again, my generation has failed in this pursuit which actually makes us a 'powerless' generation! Take us young black males for instance, we're filling these penal institutions by the thousands and to the max as if there's nothing else for us to do but commit crime! As a matter of fact, I read somewhere that there are more young black males in prison than there are enrolling in college! What's worst is the way most of us carry on while here in prison. Do you think that most brothers in here are trying to at least become better individuals? Sister, trust me, nothing could be further from the truth! There are a few who are really doing everything that they can to make this incarceration their last, but the majority of the guys here spend much of their time on the recreation yard playing sports. Those who are not playing sports, can generally be found in front of the television watching 'rap' or 'R/B' music videos. Don't get me wrong, now, I like the music videos too, but I can read and write, as well as hold a conversation without cursing or using 'street slang' while in the presence of the intellectuals!"

S.F.: "Kareem, I know exactly where you're coming from because I had another friend of mine who was incarcerated in a state institution. Whenever he would write me, I literally would hate to read his letters because he couldn't spell worth nothing which would make it hard for me to understand what he was trying to convey. I would think to myself, with the time that he got, he ought to be trying to get educated!"

Kareem: "So, you feel me? This is why I feel that it's my duty and purpose as an individual whose eyes are open, to help bring those of my generation, like the ones just described, to take a good long hard look at themselves. They need to see what they are doing wrong and just come to their senses, moving towards a positive change. In my opinion, there's nothing that we can't do, when we put our mind(s) to it."

S.F.: "You are exactly right and I want to thank you for your insight shared in this interview, as well as the truth, concerning some of your life and the lies that this Government convicted you and your co-conspirators on. Now I know for myself that the 'West Charlotte Posse' was a made up street gang by those in authority working for the Government! I feel in my heart that if this Government would fabricate you guys being the 'menaces' that they in fact claimed you all were, at the expense of you guys having to be away from society and your love ones for long stretched of time, what wouldn't this Government do? You all were young boys back in 1992, at the time of your arrest, as you, yourself Kareem, alluded to earlier on this interview. Most of you were not raised in a real solid wholesome environment, where you could have somehow escaped the many negatives that were in you guys midst. Drug users and dealers were in your neighborhoods, as was violence, 'pimpin', prostitution and the like. I have read books Kareem, where the 'professionals' who studied this type of stuff, indicated that it is an individual's 'environment' that ultimately shapes the mind and life of a person. If this is so, then how can an individual, raised in a negative environment, get caught up eventually doing negative things; be fully at fault for his/her negative behavior when that's all they were in fact raised around? I just don't get it, my brother, I just don't get it. I want you to keep doing what you were doing, your day is gonna come, prison is not your destiny. I believe this with all my heart. Also, know that I am here for you, if you ever need me for anything. Lastly, is there anything that you would like to conclude with?"

Kareem: "I would like to say in closing, thank you for your undying friendship. I know that we covered a lot of things; yet, there was so much that wasn't said. However, maybe we will get to those things in the future, but I wanna say to all those who may end up reading this, live on the truth, and if possible, go to your grave having stood on the truth. Living a lie, in my opinion, is not living at all! In addition, I want all of my young brothers and sisters to know that we come from God and God is the greatest. Everything He created, He created it to solve a problem. For example: Our eyes were created to solve a problem, so were our ears. I mean, just think about it? If we didn't have eyes, we would go through life stumbling over things constantly. If we didn't have ears, we would not be able to hear beautiful words like, "I love you" from the mouth of someone who may admire and adore us. Just like our eyes and ears were created to solve a problem, so were you and I. You and I, young brother/sister, were not created by God to be "thugs," "gangsters," "drug dealers," "stick up kids," and all of that negative bullshit! Those characters were created out of circumstances that originated from low living in the hood or the so-called "ghetto!"

You and I cannot continue to slumber in this bed of negativeness any longer, especially after knowing that you and I have the ability to rise above the negative into the positive through the exercising of common sense!

I don't know the problem that Almighty God created you to solve, but you do have a purpose worth pursuing.

Personally, I never thought while I was out there in that world "thuggin" and robbing drug dealers that I would one day become an author. No one could have told me that me, writing a book, was something the Creator had placed inside me to do. I wouldn't have believed anyone telling me that. One day after coming into contact with a young bother named Kevin Bullock, who was a published author, I knew after reading his novel that I could write one. Something inside of me at that moment told me that I could. After listening to the God within me, I tried writing, discovered that I could do it. It took a lot of effort and determination, but after several months, I penned my first novel, DEATH NO EXCEPTIONS. I sent my manuscript off to a publishing company headed by a black woman by the name of Rose Jackson-Beavers, who is also a very talented writer and business woman. She liked my work and decided she would give me the opportunity that I needed to express myself in book form. With her believing in me, coupled with me believing in myself, has produced Author Kareem; a man through with thuggin and low living. The point that I'm making in my conclusion is: there is greatness in you, young brother/sister, but you have got to believe this. Then you must give yourself a fighting chance to manifest that greatness. Sometimes it takes you getting away from the negative crowd; people who are negative are contagious. These types of people will have you acting the way they act. They will have you believing that you are something or someone other than who God created you to be. God didn't create you to be a thug; He created you to be a thinker. If you can take this for what it is worth and act on it through your belief in what you know to be right, then your best days are ahead of you."

S.F.: "Enough said, soldier. Enough said."

D E A T H

NO EXCEPTIONS!

It was one thing for William Earl Holly, an ex-con four months fresh out of State prison, broke and hungry for a quick major come up, to strong arm rob Queen City dope girl on the low - Monica Sparks, taking her coke, cash, and chromed out 190 Benz. But it was altogether something different when William put his hands on her child in the process. In the eyes of Monica and her thugged-out associates it was a fatal mistake. One in which they all were determined to have William answer for. But first, William had to be found. Follow Monica as she demonstrates in no uncertain terms what being motivated by an unhealthy emotion called REVENGE can do to a mutha.

ISBN 13: 978-0-9816483-6-1

ISBN 10: 0-9816483-6-3

http://www.myspace.com/kareemtomblin

$14.95

Have you felt lost and hurt thinking that your problems were so big that they couldn't be fixed? Darrius McMillan, who is 13 years old, couldn't see the love and support he had in his life because he was so blinded by what he didn't have. While going through trials with a mother who used drugs, death and sickness, he found his strength in the love of his grandmother.

ISBN: 0-9753634-0-9
http://www.prioritybooks.com
$10.95

Sumthin' T' Say - is a collection of colorful, stimulating and electrifying articles and poetry about everyday life experiences. Everyone who reads "Sumthin T' Say will come away thinking about Rose's hard hitting articles and her electrifying poems which convey real emotions about Love, Life and Pain.

ISBN: 978-0-9816483-2-3
http://www.prioritybooks.com
$14.95

The first book from author Lydia M. Douglas outlines effective strategies and goals to help students accomplish their dreams. Relevant to students of all ages, Douglas sets out to motivate, stimulate and inspire students, parents and teachers to strive for the highest levels of achievement. Stepping Stones is an effective resource for any student – whether struggling or at the top of the class.

ISBN:
http://www.prioritybooks.com
$14.95

Reaching Higher Heights, the second book from author Lydia M. Douglas, outlines effective strategies and goals to help students accomplish their dreams. Relevant to students of all ages, Douglas sets out to motivate, stimulate and inspire students, parents and teachers to strive for the highest levels of achievement. She encourages young people to dress for success and start thinking about a saving plan for their future. It can start with small change.

ISBN: 978-0-9816483-0-9
http://www.prioritybooks.com
$11.95

You Might Need A Jacket
Hilarious Stories of Wacky Sports Parents

Behind every successful, young athlete, there is a highly-motivated parent obsessed with the idea of their son or daughter becoming a big sports' star. Earl Austin, Jr.'s latest book, You Might Need a Jacket: Hilarious Stories of Wacky Sports Parents, is dedicated to those mothers, fathers and others who go above and beyond the call of duty to ensure their children's success in the athletic arena.

You Might Need a Jacket: Hilarious Stories of Wacky Sports Parents contains nearly two hundred stories and little anecdotes, chronicling the activities of "Straitjacket Parents," a term created to describe overzealous sports' parents. Some stories may be hard to believe, but they are all true. They range from funny and cute to strange and truly bizarre. You Might Need a Jacket provides a small dose of what happens when parents' good intentions get the best of them.

ISBN: 978-0-9819913-1-3
http://www.prioritybooks.com
$14.95

STILL GHETTO
The Sequel
By Mary L. Wilson

Mary L. Wilson, Queen of the Ink Pen, returns with the highly anticipated sequel to Ghetto Luv. Join Mya and Libra once again as they battle against deception, destruction and death in the drama-filled streets of the Lou. Brazen and bold, the mistress of seduction is back and she is sexier than ever. With a major record deal, a handsome husband and a precious son, life couldn't be any better. But problems and trouble lingers near. The twists and turns that occur in this tangled tale will leave readers begging for more.

ISBN: 978-09792823-6-2
http://www.prioritybooks.com
$14.95

Ghetto Luv

Urban novel takes you straight to the 'hood and leaves you laughing

Sassy. Urban. Funny. Mary Wilson's *Ghetto Luv* is "in your face," with the cat-and-mouse game between the Keke and Libra as the backdrop. Keke is one of the most handsome brothas in the 'hood, definitely smooth when it comes to the ladies.

Neighborhood diva Libra is described as "every man's dream and every woman's nightmare." She and her two girls rule the streets, but Libra is clearly the standout of the three. She is full of spunk, confidence and street smarts - the mistress of seduction with her drop-dead gorgeous looks. Looking for the queen of St. Louis' West End? Libra holds the title and the attitude to go along with it.

The novel is soaked with brazen sex and hardcore violence. You'll understand why when you meet Libra's girlfriends.

P R I C E L E S S

BY ANN CLAY

Keisha McKenzie-Logan, a young professional, happy in her singleness, and passionate about her community finds herself caught up by standards she and her peers have decided would be the ideal mate for someone of her stature. However, when she finds herself smitten by the likes of the handsome security guard, Wendell Russell, her crusade to resist him becomes a battle she ultimately loses when she learns that everything is not always what it seems.

ISBN: 978-0979282393
http://www.prioritybooks.com

$11.95

DESTRUCTION VIA THE MIRROR IMAGE
BY STANLEY PITCHFORD

Stanley Pitchford's book is about twelve astronauts picked to explore outer space in hopes of finding a discovery interesting to mankind. Once in space, they encounter a creature on the ship. This creature is so hard to figure out that they must find the monster's weakness in order to destroy it. On this space exploration, lives are sacrificed, passion and romance erupts while blackmail attempts surface. Author Stanley Pitchford weaves an interesting and unique science fiction novel that explores outer space and shows what can happen when we attempt to address the unknown universe.

FINDING FOREVER
BY KEISHA ERVIN

Keisha Ervin returns with her first novella. *Finding Forever* is filled with drama, love, disloyalty, and hope for the future.

It is said that if you let something go and it returns, it was always yours to begin with. Does true love really exist? For Koran, it did more than eight years ago when the love of his life left without an explanation. Once brokenhearted, time heals all things and being the big baller that he is, love for him now is riding around in his expensive cars, wearing the best jewelry money can buy and staying dipped in the latest fashions, while lying back in his beautiful crib.

ISBN: 978-0-9816483-4-7
http://www.prioritybooks.com

$14.95

PriorityBooks Current Books Order Form

Indicate the number of copies of each book you wish to purchase then click the calculate button for Total.

Book Title	Copies	Price	Total
Death, No Exceptions!		$14.95	
Sumthin' T' Say		$14.95	
Ghetto Luv		$14.95	
You Might Need A Jacket		$14.95	
Lovers' Anonymous		$14.95	
Destruction Via the Mirror		$14.95	
Priceless		$11.95	
Still Ghetto		$14.95	
A Hole In My Heart		$10.95	
Stepping Stones		$14.95	
Reaching Higher Heights		$11.95	
Sub-Total:			
Shipping & Handling ($3.95 per book):			
Total:			

LaVergne, TN USA
28 December 2009
168192LV00002B/10/P

9 780981 991337